If You Were There
in 1492

ALADDIN PAPERBACKS

If You Were There in 1492

Barbara Brenner

To my friend Stanley H. Kaplan,
for his enthusiasm

ACKNOWLEDGMENTS

In writing this book, I had a wonderful support system. I'm especially grateful to: the library staff of the Marywood College Library and the Milford (Pa.) library; Sharon Cohen of the Bank Street College Library staff, who tirelessly aided me in digging up the past; my husband, Fred Brenner, whose keen artist's eye helped shape both manuscript and visual material; my daughter-in-law, Dr. Susan Milbrath, assistant curator at the Florida Museum of Natural History in Gainesville, whose knowledge of the period of exploration was so helpful; Dr. Ruth Gordon, who read and commented on the historical aspect of the manuscript and made many useful and important suggestions; and my long-time editor and friend Barbara Lalicki, who has been a guiding force in so much of my work and, as usual, played a significant role in bringing this idea to fruition.

The title page illustration shows Columbus's ships, from left to right, the *Santa Maria*, the *Pinta*, and the *Niña*.

First Aladdin Paperbacks edition September 1998

Text copyright © 1991 by Barbara Brenner

Aladdin Paperbacks
An imprint of Simon & Schuster Children's Publishing Division
1230 Avenue of the Americas
New York, NY 10020

The text for this book was set in Galliard.
The illustrations are reproductions of woodcuts, maps, and paintings of the period.
Book design by Beth Tondreau Design
Printed and bound in the United States of America
10 9 8 7 6 5 4 3 2 1

The Library of Congress has cataloged the hardcover edition as follows:
Brenner, Barbara.
If you were there in 1492 / by Barbara Brenner.—1st ed.
p.   cm.
Includes bibliographical references.
Summary: Readers take a trip back in time to learn about the culture and civilization of 15th century Europe and Spain, and the discovery of America by Columbus.
ISBN 0-02-712321-9 (hc.)
1. Columbus, Christopher—Juvenile literature. 2. Fifteenth century—Juvenile literature.
3. America—Discovery and exploration—Spanish—Juvenile literature.
[1. Columbus, Christopher. 2. Fifteenth century. 3. America—Discovery and exploration—Spanish.] I. Title
E111.B85   1991
970.015—dc20
90-24099
ISBN 0-689-82241-3

Contents

What This Book Is About

One of the first things I learned in school was that

> In fourteen hundred and ninety-two
> Columbus sailed the ocean blue.

But I could never get much of a picture of what life was like back in that famous year. What else was happening? What were they doing and thinking in 1492, anyway? And I wondered: Did people who were alive then know they were living in historic times? Did anyone say, "This is going to be an extraordinary year"?

Opposite page: Strolling masked singers:
a scene in Italy during Columbus's time

So one day I decided to go back and dig into that corner of the past. I wanted to take a look at some of the many things that happened just in that one year, particularly in Spain. I wanted to understand how it felt to be in a certain place at a certain crucial time.

This book is about what I discovered.

Barbara Brenner

The city of Genoa, Italy, around 1492

2

The World of 1492

Once upon a time it was 1492. At the beginning of that year, there may have been fewer than 400 million people in the whole world.[1] They lived crowded into cities and towns and scattered in villages. They had no refrigerators, no electric lights, no wristwatches. On average, they were shorter than we are today. And they died earlier.

If you could step into a time capsule and be beamed back to 1492, the world would seem very strange to you. And yet, some things would be the same. The size of the earth, for example. It was the same size then as now. Still, if you look at a map made in 1492, it appears smaller. And a big chunk of it is missing. That's because the mapmakers of those days had no idea that Australia and Antarctica even existed. No one knew how big Africa really was. But the most glaring mistake in those old maps is that big space between the western coast of Europe and Asia. It may be decorated with sea creatures, or mythical islands, but there's no North America and South America!

In Europe and Asia in 1492, the mapmakers didn't know that those two continents existed. They certainly didn't know that in some of these places there were large cities, where hundreds

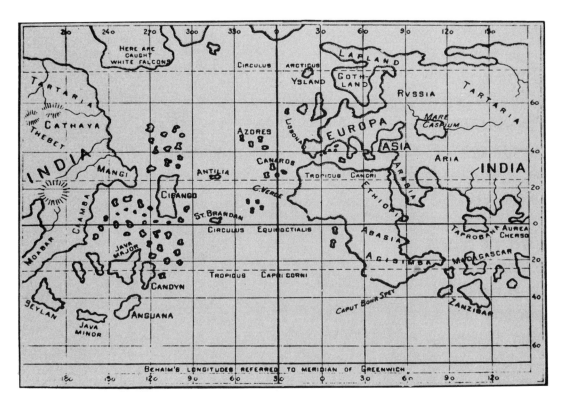

Early maps didn't show any land between Europe and the Indies.

of thousands of people lived among huge stone buildings and pyramids richly ornamented with art and sculpture. They didn't have a clue.

So what *did* people know about geography in 1492? Most educated people did know that the world was round. Merchants and sailors had some idea where Egypt and Turkey were. The European mapmakers knew about North Africa and Greece and places in the Middle East. Marco Polo had already been to China (he called it Cathay), and he knew about Japan (which he called Cipangu). So people who had seen maps knew a little bit about Asia. But the average European certainly didn't know that in Asia there were civilizations that predated hers by thousands of years. Even if she had seen the delicate blue and white porcelain dishes called "china," the average person didn't know that clocks and the compass, gunpowder, and an earthquake-measuring device had all been invented there. The Chinese were probably equally ignorant of the West. They considered Europeans barbarians.

Most ordinary people knew best the places where they lived. There were Europeans living in territories that today we call England, Scotland, France, Germany, Holland, Belgium, Portugal, Italy, and Spain. You can see these territories on the old maps, although some of them had different names and were city-states rather than countries. You can tell which were some of their important port cities: Lisbon, Portugal; Antwerp, Belgium; Alexandria, Egypt; Genoa, Italy; Bristol, England; Palos, Spain.

There were many separate states and kingdoms in Europe in 1492. But you could cross their borders without a passport. You could trade back and forth or exchange information. (It took only three days for a letter to travel from Rome to Venice.) You could go to war or compete for trade. In 1492 Spain was

competing with Portugal for territories to explore. France also wanted to be in the competition. The kingdoms and city-states of Europe wanted to open new sea routes to the faraway places that had spices and gold. They wanted to get to Persia, India, China, and Japan—the lands they called the Indies. And of course, there was the slave trade. The ancient civilizations like Greece and Rome had always taken captives as slaves. But now slavery was a business: The first African slaves had been taken in 1444 by the Portuguese, although slavery was by no means a new idea in the world.

They built ships to send to the faraway lands of spices and gold.

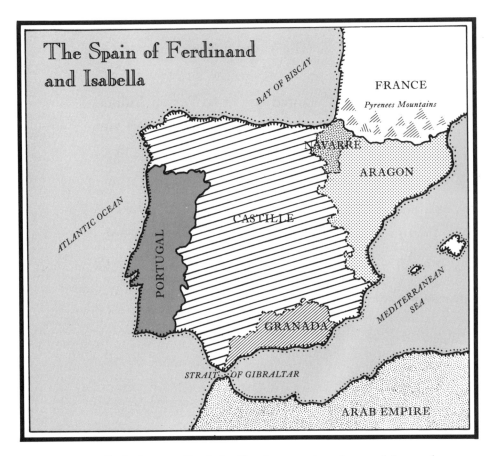

The Spain of Ferdinand and Isabella

FRANCE

BAY OF BISCAY

Pyrenees Mountains

NAVARRE

ARAGON

ATLANTIC OCEAN

PORTUGAL

CASTILLE

MEDITERRANEAN SEA

GRANADA

STRAIT OF GIBRALTAR

ARAB EMPIRE

Spain controlled almost all of the Iberian peninsula, and beyond.

Spain

Take an especially good look at Spain on the map.

Spain is part of what is still called the Iberian Peninsula. In 1492 the Iberian Peninsula looked pretty much the way it does today—like a lady's head. Portugal is a mask on the face. The skinny neck looks as if it had broken off from Africa. Between the two pieces is the Rock of Gibraltar, poking out from the sea. (You would have called it the Pillar of Hercules in 1492.) The lady's nose and mouth are in the Atlantic Ocean, which on the old maps is called the Ocean Sea. The back of her head is washed by the Mediterranean Sea. Behind and above the head are other places whose names we know as countries today: France, Italy, Germany, England.

In those days, Spain was divided into two kingdoms, Aragon and Castile. Queen Isabella governed Castile, and King

Ferdinand was the ruler of the territories of Aragon. But since these two monarchs had married each other, their two kingdoms had been wedded, too.

If you lived in the port city of Palos, Spain, that year you could have seen the ships coming in and going out. You could have watched the goods from other parts of the world arriving—the silks and spices, the sugar and the slaves. You would have seen Spain's products—the wool and leather, the iron and velvet, the raisins and dates—being put aboard. You might have seen people dressed in the colorful costumes of their native countries. You could have smelled the spices.

What you would not have been able to see or smell were the ideas in the air. The year 1492 was a time of new ideas. Explorers, writers, astronomers, artists, scientists, and musicians were all bursting with them. Ideas traveled like birds. They flew from country to country, bringing excitement with them.

If you lived in Spain or Portugal, you would have been living in one of the "hot spots" of history. It was where the exploring fever had reached its height. In 1492 the coast cities of Spain and Portugal were busy. Every day that the winds were good, ships left ports with romantic names like Palos and Cádiz, Lisbon and Cartagena. Guided by the maps and the star charts produced by the mapmakers, they sailed to Africa and the Middle East and down the coast of Africa. Spain alone had a thousand merchant ships. In all the countries of Europe, exploring was in the air. But in Spain and Portugal in 1492, it had become almost a mania.

According to his own accounts, Christopher Columbus was born in Genoa, Italy. He retained a strong feeling for the place. At one point, while in Spain, he said, "Although my body is here, my heart is always there."

When Columbus was growing up, Genoa was a bustling port city. It's easy to understand how a young boy living there could have caught sea fever. By the time Columbus was a young adult, he had already been on several long voyages, once possibly as far as Iceland.[2] He had also worked as a mapmaker. One way or other, Columbus must have looked at the Atlantic Ocean many times, and he knew its currents. It's not surprising that he came up with the notion that it was possible to reach the Indies by going west across the "Ocean Sea."

Columbus first took his idea to King John of Portugal, who, he knew, had his own personal mapmakers attached to his court. The king turned the idea down. King John seems to have been more interested in discovering an eastward route to the Indies, one that went around Africa. Besides, he thought Columbus talked too much.[3]

The scholars vetoed Columbus's plan.

A Traveler in Spain

Imagine for a few minutes that you're traveling through Spain in 1492. There are no cars or trains. People travel on foot or by mule. You're traveling by mule. But imagine that your animal can quickly whisk you around the country.

You cross into Spain from France, over the mountains of the Pyrenees. It's a hard way, going over the Pyrenees. They're rugged and snow-covered most of the year. You can see why very few people come this way. But you make it safely, and you enter the province of Aragon, King Ferdinand's territory. In the north of Spain you pass through forests and green hills where horses are grazing. You make your way over rough terrain, past rocky ravines and the rivers that run through them. You pass through the center of Spain, with its high mesas and its treeless hills.

The first thing you notice is that Spain does not seem as up-to-date as the country you've come from. In fact, it seems quite primitive. Don't they know about all the new things in Europe? Most of the ordinary houses of northern and central Spain are still made of rammed earth or mud. In many towns, the streets are not paved with stones, as they are in some parts of France and England. It's the dry season, and your mule kicks up clouds of dust on the dry roads.

Your nose notices that the bigger the town, the more garbage. In the larger cities you ride through, the sewage in the streets forms a river of black slime. You steer your mule away from it. Meanwhile you keep your eyes open for the roving bands of robbers that you've heard about.

You head your mule south. Soon you're in the country again. You pass castle after castle. These are the fortresses of the nobles who rule little pieces of Spain. They look somewhat forlorn, these castles. Many of them have cracks in them. Some are abandoned, because by this time Ferdinand and Isabella have taken the castles away from nobles who are not taking proper care of their lands and people. But some castles are being re-paired. You see a particularly beautiful castle-fortress (called an *alcázar*) on a hill in Segovia. A passerby tells you that it is the castle in which Queen Isabella grew up. It's her favorite. She

Queen Isabella's favorite castle

still uses it when she travels to this part of Spain. You know then that you have crossed into the province of Castile. You cross a wide river, over a new bridge. All this new construction is by order of King Ferdinand and Queen Isabella. The monarchs are sprucing up Spain. Before they are finished they will have built 700 new bridges.

By this time your mule is tired, and so are you. You see a sign for an inn. "*Posada*," it says. You step inside. This is not at all like the country inns of France that you are used to. It's clear to you right away that in 1492 the inns of Spain are not noted for their elegance. Now you know why one traveler from France said that the pigpens of France were better than the inns of Spain![4]

You are not too impressed with the cleanliness of the place. There are dirt walls and the barest minimum of dishes. You are told that the inn does not supply food, only a place to sleep! You are offered something to drink out of a cracked clay pitcher. You refuse. Seeing the dirty straw beds makes you itchy. And you don't like the way people in the room are looking at your money pouch. You are right to be concerned. But you realize that inns are few and far between. And you have no guarantee that the next one will be any better.

Besides, you're too tired to go on. You decide to make the best of it. You see to it that your mule is fed and you buy some bread and goat cheese from a fellow traveler. You sleep with your moneybag under your head.

The next day you continue to make your way south. You are heading toward the Mediterranean Sea and the Moorish part of Spain.

The weather is warmer. As you travel you see horses grazing in the rich pastures. You see flocks of sheep in the green valleys. Sometimes there are as many as 30,000 on one ranch. You begin to see olive groves and citrus groves and orchards of pome-granates and dates. Many of these farms, you notice, belong to Arabs—or Moors, as they are called in Spain. Many of the Moors are farmers, and they are famous for their gardens. You stop at one of these orchards, and the Arab farmer offers you a lunch of wild honey, dates, and bread, and a drink of water for your mule. Even though you are a stranger, the Arab is bound by his Islamic religion to offer you hospitality.

You move on refreshed. You pass through Seville, a city on the Guadalquivir River. Here, if you are very lucky, you may see Amerigo Vespucci, working as an outfitter of ships.

After Seville, you continue on your journey and arrive at Granada. Here you can see the Moorish influence everywhere. These Arabs are famous for their tile work and for their metal filigree tools and gates. The Spanish people have copied their art; you can see some of the Moorish style in many of the buildings of Spain. You notice that even the Christian churches and the Jewish synagogues reflect some of the architecture of the Moors. This mixture of Arab and Spanish styles is being called "Isabelline," in honor of Queen Isabella.

It is clear that, like other places in Europe, Spain shows the influence of the different people who originally settled there: Romans, Visigoths, Celts, Arabs, Jews. But by 1492 these people have intermarried. Spain has become a sort of melting pot. Everywhere you go you see the influence of many cultures. Traveling on your whirlwind tour through Spain in 1492, you see blond and blue-eyed, dark-haired and dark-eyed, light- and dark-skinned people. You get the sense that the life-styles of Jews, Christians, and Muslims are in some ways alike and in some ways quite different. To see if this is true, you will have to stay in Spain awhile.

 Christopher Columbus traveled to Spain in 1486. But he didn't cross the Pyrenees. Instead, he came into Spain through Portugal, where he was living at the time. He did travel by mule, but he didn't stay in dirty *posadas*. When Columbus left home he carried with him letters of introduction from people in high places. So he usually managed to get an invitation to stay at a nobleman's castle or at some rich man's home in a large city. Being a widower, he traveled with his young son, Diego. He stayed at the monastery of Rábida, near Palos, and left his son there in the care of the monks while he went off to talk with Isabella and Ferdinand about his great plan to sail west to the Indies.

Columbus left his son with the monks and went off to see Ferdinand and Isabella.

The Moors

If you were in Granada in January of 1492, you would have seen the surrender of the last Arab sultan of Spain.

The Spanish Arabs, the Moors, had been in Spain for over 700 years. They had originally come across the Straits of Gibraltar from Morocco, in North Africa. When the rest of Europe was still in the Dark Ages, the Moors had already established a rich culture whose capital was the Spanish city of Córdoba. Among these Arabs were famous explorers, traders, astronomers, artists, and doctors. But they were also, like many other peoples of that time, warriors and conquerors. They controlled Spain by the sword. They fought among themselves and were merciless to their enemies. They did, however, manage to get along with the Jews, whose culture was close to theirs in many ways.

Opposite page: You can still visit the beautiful Alhambra palace.

Religious tolerance was in short supply everywhere in those times. Spanish Catholics despised the Islamic religion of the Arabs. They thought of the Moors as heretics and infidels. When they had the chance, they made war against the followers of the religion of Islam. They tried to convert them. If that didn't work they tried to kill them. Slowly, over hundreds of years of on-and-off war, the Spanish managed to drive the Moors south. Finally there was only one Arab kingdom left in Spain—Granada. It was a walled city on a hill. Its fortress-palace was the Alhambra, a masterpiece of Moorish architecture that is still considered one of the wonders of the world.

The Alhambra reflected the Arab love of beauty. It was decorated with baths and fountains, and its cool, tiled courtyards were filled with stone sculpture. It had intricately carved pillars and windows. There was poetry written on the walls. Moroccan leatherbound books filled the library.

At the height of the Moorish culture, Granada had a population of 40,000. But by 1492 many of the Arabs had already left or been forced to convert to Christianity so they could live in other places in Spain. The sultan of Granada, whose name was Abdallah, was under siege by Spanish soldiers. The Spaniards had built a fort right below his city. He could see it from the Alhambra. He knew the Spanish intended to starve him out. They had also captured his son and were holding him as a hostage. Abdallah—or Boabdil, as the Spanish called him —had to surrender. The best he could do was bargain. He made a deal with Ferdinand and Isabella that gave the Arabs the right to continue to live in Spain. He tried to make a similar deal for his friends the Jews. The monarchs wouldn't agree to it.

Imagine being there on that dramatic day in 1492. You could have seen bearded Abdallah, mounted on a black horse, ride out of the fortress-city. You would have seen his servants seal the door behind him. That was Abdallah's order—that no one would pass through that door again. You would have watched him dismount and give the keys to the city to Ferdinand and Isabella. Then you would have seen him mount his horse again and ride slowly toward the rugged mountains of his Spanish exile. You might even have seen him pause to take one last look backward, at the place known today as the "Last Sigh of the Moor."

 **Christopher Columbus was present at the surrender of Granada. He was there to keep an appointment with Isabella and Ferdinand, to talk to them about financing his voyage west to the Indies—again. In 1492 Christopher Columbus was over forty years old. His blond-red hair had turned completely white. He was tired, but he still hadn't given up his dream. Little did he know, as he stood there that day, that the following day the Catholic monarchs would finally agree to his plan.**

Abdallah's surrender to Ferdinand and Isabella signaled the final defeat of the Moors.

Food and Clothing

I f you were an ordinary citizen living in Spain in 1492, you would have eaten a very spare (and unbalanced) diet. Two meals a day was the general rule. And if you came from a poor household, you would have eaten bread, bread, and more bread. Maybe a thin cabbage soup to go with it. Perhaps a little fruit in season.

No one would have urged you to eat your vegetables, because vegetables were few and far between. Green vegetables were almost unheard of. No one in Europe had ever seen a potato or a tomato.[5] As for desserts, there weren't any. The only sweet that most people ever had was honey, and that came from the bees, not from a store. You might have drunk a little goat's milk, ale, or light wine, even as a child. There was very little pure water to be had, and there were no glasses to drink from. Instead, you would probably have drunk from a clay goblet.

No one ate as much meat as we eat today. Rich people usually ate the game and fish that was hunted for sport on their lands. But poor people seldom had the chance to hunt. Most ordinary farmers needed their cattle for milk, their sheep for wool, and their pigs to sell at the market. If you were lucky enough to get a whole animal to eat, you might pickle it in brine or salt it down to keep it from going bad. Fish was dried and salted. Meat was usually served spiced with cloves, cinnamon, nutmeg, allspice, ginger, and pepper. The spices helped cover up the fact that the meat had often been hanging a little too long.

In Spain, what you ate depended somewhat on where you lived—north or south. In southern Spain so much fruit grew over such a long season that people did very little for their meals other than to gather olives, fruits, and berries and grow cabbages and grains for bread. If you were a southerner, you might have even been scornful of the "heavy" diet of the people of the north, who ate meat more often. A famous doctor living in southern Spain at that time described what he thought was an ideal meal: "a pot full of garlic seasoned with olive oil, and cabbages cooked in it, and bread."

A dinner party of 1492 tended to be sloppy.

If food was crude in Spain in 1492, so were table manners. And this sloppy state of affairs persisted for some time. Around 1550 an Italian finally wrote a book of manners. His rules give you some idea of what you would have been doing at the table:

"You should take care, as far as you can, not to spit at meal-times. . . .

"It is not polite to scratch yourself when you are seated at table. . . . It is also bad manners to clean your teeth with your napkin."

And finally: "When you blow your nose, you should not open your handkerchief and inspect it, as though pearls and rubies had dropped out of your skull."[6]

We can begin to get a picture of what it was like at a typical dinner table in Spain.

If you were there, what would you have been wearing?

As a child, you would have worn the same kind of clothes as your parents. Men wore tunics and women wore dresses of rough homespun. Most common folks had only a few garments, and no one changed clothes very often. They also didn't bathe, so the smell would have been pretty strong around that dinner table, and it wouldn't have been only the spicy food.

If you were visiting a wealthy household, the scene would have been somewhat different. Spanish nobles and their children wore silks and laces imported from other countries. The men wore colored stockings, and around that time one fashion was to have each leg a different color. Men also wore elegantly styled soft caps. This finery was replaced by a helmet and body armor when the nobles went to war.

Women wore skirts and bodices of velvet, with contrasting color inserts of different fabrics. Italy was the fashion capital of the world in 1492, and rich Spanish women copied Italian fashion. Blond hair was in style in 1492; some women bleached their hair by spreading it out in the sun. But they were careful to shield their faces from the sun's rays. White skin was highly valued. Women wore gold chains around their necks. They pasted beauty marks on their faces. But in spite of all this show of elegance, the smell at an upper-class dinner party might have been the same as that around a peasant table. (The Arabs had already introduced the idea of a regular bath in Spain, but only a few Spaniards had taken it up as a custom.) Perhaps this was why perfume was used so freely among the rich and well dressed.

It was fashionable to bleach your hair in the sun.

31

Christopher Columbus probably wore the tunic, colored hose, and soft velvet cap of the times. In paintings of him that were done later, he is often shown wearing a long cloak, which was also typical. The hats he and his men wore are mentioned in his ship's log, because the native people he encountered admired them and he traded them some of the hats. As for his food habits, the explorer appears not to have been very interested in fancy food. But he did see to it on his voyages that his men had as good a diet as he could give them. He made sure that they had fresh fruit aboard on the first voyage. They also took with them dried beans, salt pork, sardines, biscuits, raisins, olive oil, wheat flour, cheeses, wine, vinegar—and a whole basket of garlic!

Sickness and Health

Y ou were lucky to be healthy in 1492. There were plenty of ways in which to get sick—from stagnant water, rotten food, bad diet, and the filth and garbage that were a breeding place for germs. If you did catch something, there were no antibiotics and no way of keeping sick people from infecting one another. Diseases didn't even stay in one country. Trading ships carried rats and germs from port to port. They spread sickness from one city to another. In fact, in 1492 Europe was still recovering from a plague that had taken half its population.

There was no protection from a plague, either. But, as in other ages, people tried to control what they feared with charms and magic. In your family you might have tried to ward off a plague by putting a small bird or a spider in a room before you went in. Or you might have tied a billy goat outside your door. Or perhaps you took a piece of paper inscribed with a prayer, folded it seven times, and swallowed it (on an empty stomach for best results).

If you were unlucky enough to get sick after all that, you would have taken yourself to an apothecary, which was like a drugstore. There you would buy a little box of herbs. You'd take a different one every day—perhaps rue on Monday, camomile on Tuesday, hyssop on Wednesday, and so on. And you'd hope to get well before the week was out. In any case, ordinary people in most parts of Europe didn't see a doctor or go to a hospital, although there were some dispensaries and hospitals operating by that time. (China already had a fairly sophisticated hospital system.)

Camomile was one of the herbs used to treat upset stomach.

Attendants and doctors cared for rich people who were ill.

By contrast, kings and queens and nobles in Europe often had their private physicians. These doctors had been educated in medicine at a university. In Spain, many of them were Arabs or Jews. For kings as well as for commoners, however, the cure was sometimes worse than the disease. Very often a doctor would "bleed" a patient, hoping that the disease would leave the body with the bad blood. Too often the patient died.

 Christopher Columbus and the later Spanish explorers didn't know it, but they brought disease to the places they explored. The people living there had no resistance to European illnesses, and they died by the thousands. But the explorers themselves were not immune to disease. It is probable that syphilis was unknown in Europe until the explorers brought it back with them from the New World.[7]

Kings and Queens

B ack in the fifteenth century, most countries were ruled by a king or queen or the prince of a noble family. Some kings and queens did more for their people than others. Henry the Navigator, who ruled Portugal in the middle of the fifteenth century, promoted sailing and exploration and established a school of navigation. Before and after 1492, the ruling family of Florence, Italy—the Medici—was known for its support of artists and musicians.

Kings and queens usually ruled for life. They had complete power over their subjects. If you were living back then, you wouldn't have thought this was unfair. The idea of people voting for a leader would never have occurred to you. In fact, if you lived in Spain, you might have considered yourself lucky. Unlike many of the kings and queens of that day, Ferdinand and Isabella didn't collect taxes from their subjects in order to live in high style. They lived simply and paid close attention to building up their country. Under their rule, Spain stopped being a country of noble families who controlled huge land holdings and who fought among themselves. Instead, it became a united country under one central government. Some of the feudal landholdings were broken up, and the castles were turned over to the crown. Others became fortresses of royal power pledged to defend the territory of the king and queen. Still other noble families were invited to live at court.

In 1492, there were ten children of noblemen living at the court of Spain. If you had been born into a noble family, you might have been one of them. You would have grown up with the prince and the princesses. That would have been a good life for you. In some ways, you might have had a better life than the heirs to the throne. Royal children were kidnapped, held for ransom, even murdered. In many cases they were held as hostages in wars. Many of today's fairy tales are based on true stories of these princes and princesses of olden days who were locked in towers by jealous brothers, sisters, or other relatives or who simply disappeared.[8]

If you lived at court you would have seen a lot of King Ferdinand and Queen Isabella. You might have traveled with

Queen Isabella

King Ferdinand

the royal party as they made their rounds of the kingdom. A
boy would have gone hunting with the king and taken part in
the royal jousting tournaments. This was training for war, so
that you could defend Spain. You would have found King

Ferdinand a good role model. He was a fearless warrior and a shrewd politician. A boy who watched the king could learn some valuable lessons in politics.

A girl at the court of Ferdinand and Isabella also learned many things. The queen herself was extremely well educated. She read Latin, knew how to play the lute, and kept up with the latest cultural trends.[9] Isabella saw to it that the daughters as well as the sons of the nobles living at court had the same tutors that her children had. If you lived at court, she would personally have taken charge of your education. She would have introduced you to some of the new books that were coming out of Italian and Belgian printing houses. The queen had a library of over two hundred books—a large collection in those days. Perhaps she would have let you read some of them.

When you saw the queen, you would have noticed that she dressed very modestly. She usually wore very little jewelry. Of course, kings and queens had to dress up sometimes, if only to impress noble visitors. Isabella certainly owned fancy clothes. You might have been there on one state occasion when she is reported to have worn a skirt of ruffled green velvet with an overdress of crimson brocade and a ruby-and-pearl necklace. With her auburn hair, the queen of Spain must have been a memorable sight!

But supposing you came from an ordinary Spanish family. What, then, were your chances of meeting the queen? Actually, they were pretty good. If you had a complaint about taxes or wanted to protest a crooked land deal, you could have asked for an audience. If it were granted, you would have come, waited your turn, and then, kneeling or curtsying before her, told your story.

Isabella was a very unusual queen. Instead of conducting all her royal business from one of her many castles, she traveled all over her kingdom. Sometimes she went with the armies. During wars, she organized supplies for the troops and even saw to the wounded. In peacetime she rode great distances to appear personally in the local courts and to listen to her subjects. In fact, Isabella traveled around so much that each one of her five children was born in a different city.[10]

During these visits, nothing escaped the queen's attention. She made notes on the smallest details. She would tuck these scraps of paper in her sleeve and pull them out at the proper time and discuss them. However, there was one subject that was not open for debate in the court of Isabella and Ferdinand. That subject was religion. The queen was deeply religious. She spent hours every day in prayer. After a while her religious feelings seemed to take over her whole life. She wanted Spain to be entirely Christian. She wanted her Jewish and Islamic subjects to turn Catholic. And she insisted that they forget all of their former customs. Isabella's fanaticism was the cause of the expulsion of the Jews, one of the saddest events of 1492.

Christopher Columbus first had an audience with Ferdinand and Isabella in 1486. They were interested in his scheme for reaching the Indies and agreed to think about it. But when they asked a group of scholars to evaluate it, the scholars all said it couldn't be done.

They said his distance calculations were way off, as indeed they were. It was not until six years later that Isabella and Ferdinand agreed to finance his expedition. Some historians feel that Isabella agreed because Columbus promised to convert all the people in the Indies to the Catholic Church. It seems clear that Christopher Columbus shared Isabella's religious fervor. He believed that God had appointed him to make this voyage.[11]

Education

If you were around in 1492, you might not even have known when you were born or how old you were. There's a good chance you might not have been able to read or write. Most people couldn't. Merchants might make their mark to sign a paper, but they often had to get someone to tell them what they were signing. And yet there were universities in many of the large cities of Europe. (In 1492, the great astronomer Copernicus was studying at the University of Cracow, in Poland.)

In Spain alone nine universities were opened between 1472 and 1526. Some of them were open to women, and a few even had female professors. University education was an idea supported by Queen Isabella,[12] probably because Spain lagged notoriously behind other countries in scholarship. There were only two or three professors at the University of Salamanca who even spoke Latin. Unfortunately, it was the privileged citizens who went to the universities. Other folks had to settle for learning a trade or being educated by the clergy.

If you were a boy in Spain, you might have gone to an ABC school. There you would have learned your first lessons from a hornbook. The hornbook was a piece of parchment backed by a board. On it were written the Lord's Prayer, the alphabet, and a few basic rules of grammar. If you did well, you moved along and passed the hornbook down to a younger brother. If you didn't learn your hornbook lessons well, you could have expected a flogging.[13]

If you were a merchant's son, you might have had a tutor or gone to an elementary school and then to university. You'd have been there for about seven years, or until you had become a master of your subject or craft. That's when you would have given a lecture on your "masterpiece." If you weren't so well-to-do, you might have become an apprentice and spent the same amount of time learning a craft, such as weaving. After many years of hard work and tests of various kinds, you might have been accepted in a craft guild. In that case, you would have taken your place in the street of the weavers, or cobblers, or blacksmiths. Or you might have entered a monastery, to be

Students who didn't learn their lessons were flogged.

educated by the monks or priests for a possible career in the priesthood.

Wars, big and small, were part of everyday life. In that one year of 1492, England invaded France, Turkey invaded Hungary, the sultan of Delhi, in India, annexed Bihar, and Spain defeated the Moors after five hundred years of on-and-off war.[14] So it was no wonder that most boys received training in warfare. The sons of kings and noblemen's sons went into battle with their fathers at the age of twelve or thirteen. Younger boys of all classes played at war and practiced jousting with sticks. When they got old enough, the ordinary lads of the countryside could try their hands with the crossbow and the longbow.

In 1492 a boy who had a taste for adventure could be a soldier or sailor and see the world. Girls, on the other hand, didn't go anywhere, unless they were the daughters of royalty or came from upper-class families. If you had been one of Queen Isabella's daughters, you would have been among the most educated women in Europe at that time.[15] You would have had a private tutor and been able to speak and read Latin as well as your native Castilian. In addition, you would have learned fine sewing and how to play an instrument.

If you were a merchant's daughter, you might have been sent to a nunnery to be educated. But poorer girls received no ed-

Queen Isabella was interested in the education of women.

ucation. They worked hard at home and were married off early. If you had been a ten-year-old girl in the year 1492, you would have already been prepared to run a household. If you were fifteen, chances are you would already have been married. Until marriage, you might have helped your father in his work. Some sculptors, painters, and other craftsmen who had daughters instead of sons used them as assistants. One printer of the fifteenth century, Christophe Plantin of Antwerp, Belgium, described how his five young daughters were trained to correct page proofs in several languages. They started at age four. But one of the girls, he complained, was slow. She was eight and she still couldn't seem to get the hang of it![16]

 Christopher Columbus had a good education. But it is not clear how he acquired it. In those days, the son of a wool weaver wasn't likely to go to a university, and yet Columbus spoke and wrote Spanish, Portuguese, and Latin. Maybe he had taught himself to read and write so he could work in his brother's chart-making shop. He had probably taught himself Latin so he would be able to read books about navigation and travel.

Arts and Entertainment

In the Spain of 1492, few occasions were complete without music. You would have heard it everywhere. From the windows of castles, you might have heard the sound of a lute. In the villages and on the terraced hillsides you could see muleteers plucking mandolins. You would hear songs of romance and adventure. If you couldn't afford an instrument yourself you could always sing in-part songs (choral songs sung in harmony). You could join a choir or just sing at parties. Most people could read music if they could read words. There were already ballets and musical shows as well as street fairs to go to. And of course one of the favorite forms of entertainment in Spain was the bullfight.

But if you couldn't attend one of these events, you entertained yourself. An evening's relaxation in 1492 might have revolved around a little homemade musical entertainment, and maybe some gambling and cards. Both grown-ups and children played cards and chess. They also bowled and played tennis. If you were a child back then, you might have played a version of blindman's buff.[17] Falconry was a popular sport all over Europe and in parts of Asia and Africa. The hawks' bells used on the feet of captive hawks and falcons were sold in every market.

An evening's entertainment might include a game of chess.

As for art, there were plenty of religious paintings and handsome wood carvings, called *retablos*, in the Catholic churches of Spain. Much of the most beautiful sculpture was in the tombs and mausoleums. This art was very different from what you would have seen in synagogues and Arab buildings, because Jews and Moors were prohibited by their religions from depicting the human figure.

If you wanted to be a painter or sculptor you looked to Italy. In Italy a renaissance (rebirth) of the arts and the sciences was taking place. Italy was becoming the most civilized and cosmopolitan place in Europe.

As a budding artist visiting Italy in 1492, you could have seen the work of Verrocchio, Botticelli, Bramante, and Ghirlandaio. You might have gone hoping to attract the attention of Lorenzo de Medici, a famous patron of the arts. If you did, he might have invited you to live at his palace and study art by copying his wonderful art collection. There you would have met a seventeen-year-old artist named Michelangelo, who was already creating great works.

Lorenzo de Medici died some time in 1492. If you arrived in Italy after his death, you might have tried to become an apprentice to a well-known painter. If you were very lucky, you might have been taken on as an assistant by the greatest of them all—Leonardo da Vinci. In 1492 Leonardo da Vinci was forty years old, about the same age as Christopher Columbus and Queen Isabella. His painting and sculpture was already the talk of Europe. Working for Leonardo, you would have learned how to mix powdered tempera paint with eggs. You might even have experimented with a new method—mixing paint with oil.

Working under da Vinci, you would have learned much besides painting, sculpting, and drawing. Leonardo was interested in all aspects of the world and liked to try new things. He collected fossils, studied live animals, and designed military weapons, buildings, and toys. You might have helped him with

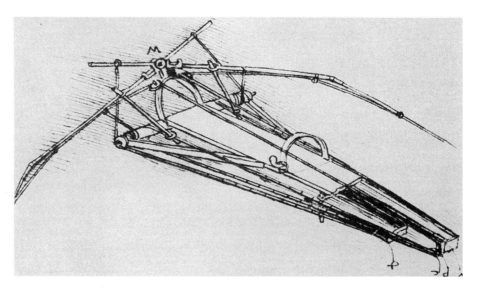

Leonardo da Vinci's sketch for a flying machine

the "Paradise Festival" he designed for the duke of Milan. It featured a great domed model of the heavens, with planets revolving in their orbits and gods and goddesses floating down among them. If you worked for Leonardo in 1492, you would have seen him complete a design for a flying machine.

If you were lucky enough to become Leonardo da Vinci's assistant, you would have had the chance to see a great deal of his work. This is an experience you could not have today, because only twelve of his paintings have survived the centuries. One of them is probably the most famous painting in the world—*La Giaconda*, or as we know it, the Mona Lisa.

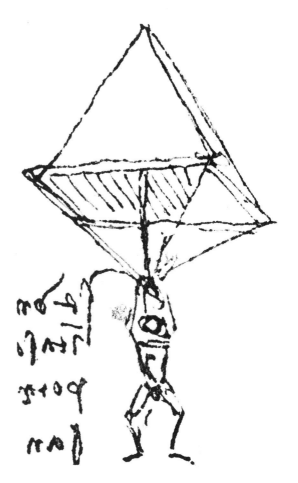

Leonardo also designed a parachute.

Books and Printing

I f you were around in 1492, you might have had a chance to read one of the new Spanish romance novels. It was called *Prisoner of Love*, and it was a best-seller back then. Of course, you would have had to read Latin, because most of the books of the time were written in that language. Fortunately, that same year a man named Antonio de Nebrija wrote the first Latin-Spanish dictionary. This made it easier for Spaniards to get the full meaning of the literature they read.

There was a good reason why the book business was booming that year. Mass printing had become a real profession. The first encyclopedia had just been published, and more than two hundred cities in Europe had print shops. Books could now be set in movable type, rather than being laboriously copied by hand. Instead of one copy of a book, there could be hundreds.

At about the same time someone had invented a process for making paper. It was by no means the first invention of paper. The Egyptians, the Chinese, and the Arabs had all tried their hands at it. But this was a quicker, cheaper way to make paper from linen rags. The rags were boiled and then beaten to a pulp. This mash was then poured into a shallow wire frame with a wire bottom. The excess water drained out through the bottom,

Paper was made from linen rags.

From one of Columbus's books showing the pointing finger

and the rest was left to dry into a sheet. Books could be printed much more cheaply on this surface than on the costly vellum made from animal skins. And it lasted a very long time. In fact, there are books still in existence today that were made of this kind of paper, in spite of the fact that in 1492 a man named Giovanni Triteniro had said that printed books would never be as good as handwritten manuscripts. After 1492, vellum continued to be used for special, one-of-a-kind maps and presentation books. But the book with paper pages was used for mass printing.

Your life would have been changed considerably by the fact that books were more widely available. If you could afford it and could read, you could now own books. You could share the ideas of people living in distant parts of the world. You could read the ideas of astronomers, explorers, poets, and novelists. Imagine the impact that would have had on your life in 1492. Even if you never left Spain, you could now read about life and ideas in other places.

Christopher Columbus was a great reader. He seems to have been particularly interested in everything that was published on the subject of navigation and geography.

Some of Columbus's books have been preserved in the Biblioteca Columbina in Seville, Spain. Among them are Cardinal d'Ailly's *Imago mundi*, Pliny's *Natural History*, the Latin edition of *The Travels of Marco Polo*, and the *Almanaque de navigacion*, by Abraham Zacuto. Some of the books have the Admiral's marginal notes and a pointing hand drawn on the page to call attention to a sentence.

By 1492, books were widely available.

Crime and Punishment

In some ways, 1492 was a cruel time. Punishment for all crimes was swift and nasty. Often people were tried and then hanged right on the spot if they were found guilty. Death by hanging was common, and gallows were sometimes set up in a town square at a moment's notice. Trials often took place when the king, queen, or ruling prince was coming to a city. The monarchs would sometimes stay to watch justice carried out. In many countries, hanging was the most merciful death you could expect in 1492. Almost anywhere in Europe, you could be burned at the stake, drawn and quartered, or skinned alive. You could have your head cut off. Even if you managed to escape being killed, your life could be ruined. Crimes like stealing were punished by having a hand cut off, or a foot. In any big city you could see hundreds of people hobbling through the streets, serving life sentences as cripples in payment for crimes they may or may not have committed. And it was such a common sight to see the head of a convicted criminal stuck on a pike that after a while people hardly noticed anymore.

You were most likely to lose your head over a religious or political issue. Anyone whose belief was the least bit odd or different ran the risk of being accused of being a witch or of

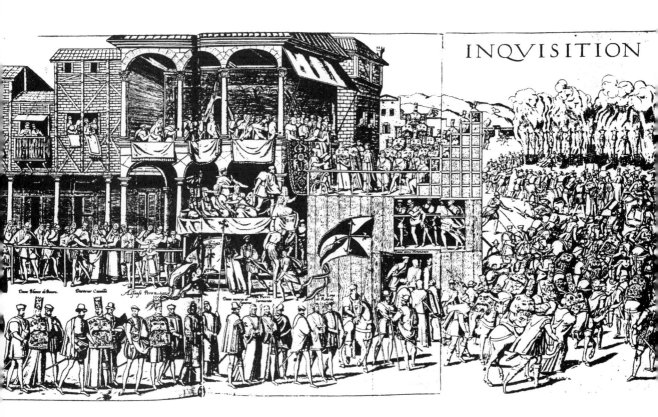

Victims of the Inquisition often were paraded through the streets before being executed.

being in league with the devil. Germany had a huge witch hunt around this time, and thousands of people were put to death. Most of them were women. If you were a woman in Germany in 1492, you were twice as likely as a man to be accused of witchcraft.[18]

Man or woman, it was hard to defend yourself once you were accused of something. Often you never saw the person who had accused you. Sometimes people were tortured until they confessed to anything. Ordinary people had no one to defend them. You weren't safe even if you were born into a noble family. The only advantage you had was that you couldn't be tortured. And you were allowed to have your head cut off instead of being hanged. But for treason or heresy against the Christian God, everyone, lord or peasant, had the same privilege of being hanged or burned.

In the year 1492 what you believed, or didn't believe, could cost you your life almost anywhere in Europe. But in Spain there was the *Inquisition*.

The Spanish Inquisition had started in 1480 to investigate cases of "heresy and lapses of faith." Isabella was responsible. The queen wanted to make Spain a totally Catholic country. She was urged on by her religious adviser, Tomas de Torquemada, and Ferdinand approved, although grudgingly at first.

Jews and Muslims began to be persecuted unless they converted to Christianity. Some of them did. But even renouncing your own religion didn't guarantee safety from persecution. A converted Jew (a *marrano*) or a converted Arab (a *Morisco*) could be hounded simply for clinging to some of his own customs.

Eventually, both the Jews and the Arabs felt the full weight of the Inquisition. But Torquemada's first target was the Jews. He carefully planted seeds of distrust against the Jews, calling on all the prejudices that he could awaken among Catholic Spaniards. His lies about Jews fell on fertile ground. Christians, forbidden by their religion to collect taxes or to lend money, had turned these jobs over to Jews. Jews became the official tax collectors and money-changers for those in power. It was easy for people to hate the tax collector.

Meanwhile, false rumors about Jews began to be passed around from mouth to mouth. *Jewish doctors carried poison in their fingernails. Jews cut the hearts out of Christian children and used them in their sacrifices.*[19] If you were a Jew your ancient customs were suspect. And a Jew who had converted to Christianity could be accused of "Judaizing," or having a "lapse of faith." How was a lapse of faith discovered? People would stand on a hillside overlooking the Jewish quarter on a Saturday, trying to spot the homes with no fires burning. The absence of a fire

Wearing a sanbenito *meant you and your family were marked forever.*

meant that the family inside was still following Jewish law, which forbids lighting a fire on the Sabbath.

By 1492 the Jews in Spain were having a terrible time. As a traveler from another country, you would have seen the evidence. Walking the streets of the cities of Seville or Cordoba, you would have known right away which people were Jews. You would have seen Jewish men, women, and children paraded barefoot through the streets, forced to wear badges or circles of cloth to set them apart from other Spaniards, as they would be forced to do under the Nazis in Germany over 400 years later. You might even have witnessed the most visible sign of the Inquisition—an *auto da fe*, or "act of faith." This was nothing more than a grisly public torture and execution. Accused people were rounded up by the Inquisition and turned over to a civil court for public trial. Anyone who wouldn't confess to "Judaizing," heresy, blasphemy, or a number of other religious sins, even under torture, was burned at the stake. Sometimes their grandparents' bodies were dug up from their graves and burned with them. Those who confessed were paraded through the streets wearing a cone-shaped hat and a yellow sack called a *sanbenito*. Black and red sanbenitos with hideous devils on them were reserved for those about to be killed.

During this terrible time, there were many priests who spoke out against the treatment of the Jews. But somehow Torquemada always had the last word. If you had been in Spain in April of 1492, you would have seen the situation come to a head. At the end of that month, the royal order was issued: All Jews were to be expelled unless they became Christians.

 **Some historians have speculated that Columbus was of Jewish ancestry and that this was the reason he was so vague about his background. It's certainly a possibility: There had been a great deal of intermarriage between Christians and Jews before it became so important in Spain to have "pure" blood. Ferdinand himself had a Jewish grandparent. But if Columbus was a *marrano*, or had Jewish ancestors, he kept it to himself.[20]**

About the same time that the Jews were ordered from Spain, Columbus negotiated the final terms of the Articles of Agreement with Ferdinand and Isabella. The monarchs agreed to all of his demands, including his wish to have golden spurs and to be called Admiral of the Ocean Sea.

The Expulsion

I f you had been in Spain in March of 1492, you would
have known about the expulsion order. And you might
have sensed something strange about it. At the same time
that Jews and *marranos* were being tried and executed under the
Inquisition, some Jews still held positions in high places. A Jew,
Isaac Abravanel, was Queen Isabella's tax collector. His son,
Judah, was the court physician. Isabella's financial adviser, Luis
Santangel, was a *marrano*, a converted Jew. If you were one of
the palace children, you would probably have seen these men.
They might have patted your head or spoken to you. Judah
Abravanel might have given you medicine for an earache.

When the news came that the Jews were to be banished from
their native land, these men and a few others were exempted
from the order. Still, Abravanel tried to speak for his Jewish

brothers and sisters. He begged the monarchs to change their minds. But Torquemada arrived at a crucial moment to make sure that Ferdinand and Isabella did not soften their hearts. Here are Abravanel's own words describing the meeting:

"I pleaded with the king many times. . . . Why do you do this to your servants? Lay on us every tribute and ransom, gold and silver, and everything that the children of Israel possess they shall willingly give to their fatherland. . . . But all in vain. . . . Like an adder that stops its ears, [the king] remained deaf to

Torquemada appeared at a crucial moment to denounce the Jews.

our appeals. The queen also . . . would not listen to our pleas. On the contrary, she argued in favor of the plan."[21]

So Abravanel and his family decided to leave Spain with the others. When the royal couple realized that they were going to lose both their doctor and their treasurer, they hatched a plot to kidnap Judah Abravanel's son and hold him hostage so that his father and grandfather would stay in Spain. Luckily, the Abravanels got wind of the plot. They spirited the child out of Spain and into Portugal with a nursemaid. But, sadly, they themselves were never able to go to Portugal. And they never saw the boy again.

Imagine for a minute what it was like to be a Jewish child in Spain in that year.

All Jews have to leave the country by the end of August. By June there are hundreds of Jewish homes for sale. Just as suddenly, the price of houses drops. Your father is forced to sell your home for a mule, your vineyard for a suit of clothes. But what does it matter? Jews are not allowed to take anything valuable out of the country.

Leaving your wordly goods is not as awful as leaving your homeland. Your people have been in Spain for a thousand years. In despair, your father goes to the cemetery and digs up the bones of your ancestors to take with you into exile. If you are a twelve-year-old girl, your family hastily arranges a marriage for you. This is done so that, in case you are separated from your family, you will go into exile under protection of a husband.

As the deadline approaches, you ask your father and mother why the family cannot become Christians so that you can all stay in Spain. In your heart you know the answer. Judaism is your religion. Besides, becoming a *marrano* will not guarantee your safety. The Inquisition persecutes *marranos*, too. Even the name is a curse; it means pig or filthy person. It is clear that no Jew or former Jew is safe in Spain.

And so you set out for the coast. More and more families join you, until there is a line of refugees as far as the eye can see. People come on foot, on donkeys, on mules, on horseback. They crowd every road leading out of Spain. Thousands of people of all ages plod along the dusty roads in the heat. You see mothers carrying babies, grandsons helping elderly grandfathers. You march in a slow procession, with the rabbis leading. You play a timbrel (tambourine) to keep up your spirits. Some children play drums and blow trumpets. Everyone sings. You see babies being born at the side of the road. You see the sick and the dying. Sympathetic Christians stand silently by the side of the road, watching. Some of them are crying. But they are forbidden to help any of you, on pain of death.

Your band of refugees heads west, toward the port of Cadiz. You are hoping to go to Africa on a ship. Other people are going to Portugal. Others will go to Italy and France. You know that once you are on the ship your troubles will not be over. You have heard tales of sickness on board, and sailors and captains who will murder Jews on the chance that they are carrying hidden gems. You are afraid. At last you arrive at the ocean. It is the first time you have ever seen it. Your mother begins to

Jews who left Spain by ship landed as far away as India.

cry. Some Jews begin to pray for a miracle, as in the Bible. But Moses does not come. The sea does not part.

According to some historians, more than 200,000 Jews were forced to leave Spain in 1492. Twelve thousand died at sea. Of those who made it, about 30,000 went to North Africa, 12,000 to France and Italy, and 90,000 to the "land of the sultan," which was Turkey. If you were a Spanish Jew living in those times, you might have ended up as far away as India.[22]

 Isaac Abravanel and Luis Santangel were two early supporters of Columbus who were of Jewish ancestry. They thought his idea of sailing west to the Indies was a good one. Luis Santangel was the man who persuaded Isabella to agree to Columbus's final terms. Both Luis Santangel and Abravanel lent money to the royal treasury for Christopher Columbus's first voyage. Both of them were forced to leave Spain in 1492. Abravanel and his family were able to get to Naples. Luis Santangel's fate is unclear. One source says he fled to France, after being burned in effigy in Spain.

The Mapmakers

<hr/>

At the end of the fifteenth century mapping was already an ancient art. People had been making maps for at least 2,000 years. If you lived in Spain, you would have known about Abraham Zacuto and the mapmakers of Majorca. On that Spanish island the chief industry was mapmaking, or cartography, and most of the mapmakers were Jewish.[23] The maps were usually made on vellum, the cured skin of unborn calves, or on gazelle hide. They were hand-painted and decorated with fancy lettering in Latin. If there was a big area that a mapmaker knew nothing about, it would be decorated with imaginary countries and creatures. Each time an explorer returned with the story of a new land, the mapmakers would put it into the newest map. That way the maps carried the new information. Unfortunately, they also carried some of the old misinformation.

In 1492 maps were in big demand. The mapmakers were busy making maps for explorers and for kings and queens to give as gifts. Because printing was now established as a profession, more people could have copies of maps. And for ordinary purposes, they could be printed on paper, and they didn't cost as much.

But, of course, a map is flat. And the world is round. No one had made a globe of the world since way back in Greek times. And those old globes were no longer in existence. Along came Martin Behaim. Martin Behaim loved maps. They were his passion and his hobby, even though he wasn't trained as a mapmaker. He thought he knew more about maps than the people who were making them. And in 1492 he persuaded his hometown of Nuremberg, Germany, to accept this excellent view of himself. The city council gave Martin Behaim seventy-five dollars to construct a globe of the world.

He started work on it immediately. The globe, which he called an *Erdapfel*, or "earth apple," was to be fifty centimeters in diameter (a little over nineteen inches). It was made of a composition material layered over a mold. Behaim hired an artist named Glockenthon to actually draw the countries on the surface and then letter more than a thousand place names. Glockenthon worked on strips of animal skins called parchment, which were then fitted and pasted onto the molded sphere. He decorated

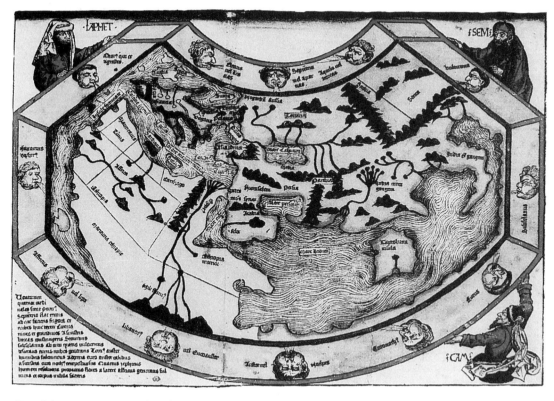

In this 1492 map, the figures represent races, or nations.

the map with 111 miniature figures of things like monsters, kings, camels, mermaids, and flags, using six different colors. When the globe was finished, it was mounted on a wooden tripod and put on display.

Martin Behaim's globe was finished in 1492. If you were around back then, you might have heard about it. It caused

Martin Behaim's globe is the oldest one still in existence.

quite a stir. But what people didn't know was that Behaim had repeated the mistakes of the earlier mapmakers. The brand-new globe showed the earth about 25 percent smaller than it actually is. The wrong sizes were now cemented to the surface of the world's first globe! Anyone looking at Behaim's globe would have thought that if you sailed west across the Atlantic Ocean from—say—Spain, you could reach the Indies before you ran out of food and water. It wouldn't be a big trip, according to his globe. It was only about 3,000 miles. And it was clear sailing. No other land in the way. That's what Behaim thought. That's what the other mapmakers thought. And that's what most people believed.

According to one historian, Antonio de Herrera, Christopher Columbus may have met Martin Behaim in Portugal.[24] It appears that Columbus was interested in seeing a "sphere" representing the world, and he once sent one to an Italian scholar named Paolo Toscanelli, along with his ideas for sailing "west to reach the east." No one knows whether he saw Behaim's globe. But he certainly studied as well as made many maps of the time before he set off on his voyage. And he took a famous mapmaker, Juan de la Cosa, along with him. If Columbus had known all the facts, he might not have gone at all. The fact is, the distance from the coast of Spain westward to Japan is over 10,000 miles.

Ships and Sailors

In 1492, many people were caught up with the idea of exploring and travel by sea. Of course, a love of the ocean was nothing new. Trade had made many cities prosperous. In fact, every year since the year 1000 the city of Venice held a special festival to celebrate its "marriage" to the ocean. Venetian shipbuilders would build a state ship just for the occasion. The upper deck of the vessel was always decorated with crimson and cloth of gold. Famous artists would design costumes and parade floats for the occasion. Princes and princesses would come from all over Europe to watch the doge, the head of the Venetian state, cast a ring into the water to symbolize Venice's marriage to the sea.

If you were an adventurous lad of ten or twelve living in those times, you too might have caught sea fever. Of course, there

Tales of sea monsters abounded.

were those who would have tried to talk you out of it. Some people still believed that if a ship sailed past a certain point it would be sucked under by wild winds and whirlpools. And let's not forget that it was only twenty years since two Italians had been burned at the stake for saying that the world was round.

If you went to sea (despite warnings) you might have sailed on a caravel, a graceful Mediterranean-style ship with triangular sails that had been invented by the sailors of Henry the Navigator. Or you could have sailed on a heavier, square-rigged *nao*, like the *Santa María*. You would most likely have shipped on as a gromet, or cabin boy. And your first job would probably have been to "learn the ropes." Ropes were the heart of the sailing ships. They moved the sails and controlled the ship's direction and speed. The rigging was entirely made of rope, and there was a rope that held the anchor. To prevent leaking, the seams of the boat were stuffed with shredded rope, called oakum. Shredding oakum for caulking might have been one of your jobs as a gromet.

Another of your jobs might have been that of timekeeper. It's important on a ship to know how long it's taking to go a certain distance and how much time has passed. But in 1492 clocks like the ones we know hadn't been invented. The clocks made at that time were useless on a moving ship. In fact, ship clocks didn't appear until the eighteenth century.

Sometimes calculations were made from the position of the stars. But sailors also used a sandglass. It looked like the timer we use for eggs or for certain board games. The *ampolleta*, as it was called, was turned every half hour to mark the passage of time and to tell sailors when to change shifts on the watch. As a gromet, you might very well have been expected to "turn the glass." As you did so, you'd sound a bell. Two bells represented the passage of one hour. Eight bells meant that the

Many sailors thought the compass was a devilish invention.

four-hour watch was over and it was time for a new person to come on duty.

Turning the glass was a big responsibility. If you fell asleep or forgot to turn the glass, the calculations on the ship were thrown off.[25]

Telling time by a sandglass seems pretty primitive. But so were other aspects of sailing in 1492. For example, if you were on a fifteenth-century ship, you would have seen the ship's speed measured by throwing a log chip into the water from the bow, or front. The time it took for the ship to pass the chip from bow to stern was written down in a book, which later came to be known as the ship's "log." The log was used to help record the course of the ship.

Some navigators had instruments such as the quadrant to measure the position of the ship in relation to stars whose position they knew. And by this time in history the compass (which was called a "wind rose") was in wide use, although many sailors still didn't trust or understand it. Your first time at sea, you too may have thought that jumping needle was a form of witchcraft.

With the aid of a sandglass, a log chip, and a compass, a sea captain could figure out in what direction he was going and at what speed. He could plot a course this way; it was known as dead reckoning. But you also had to know the wind and be able to "read" the other natural signals: the kinds of clouds forming, the color of the sky, even how the birds were flying. It wasn't easy: One historian, Ernle Bradford, compares it with trying to cross a familiar room in the dark without touching anything.

The leadsman's job was to find out how deep the water was at a given spot. He swung a lead sinker on a knotted rope into the water. The last knot left on the surface of the water told the depth. And if tallow were stuffed into the hole in the sinker, it could pick up samples from the ocean bottom and tell you whether you were in an area of mud, coral, or shale.

If you were a cabin boy in 1492, you would have found sailing uncomfortable, if not downright dangerous. You would have lived on salted meat and beans, with only wine and stale water to drink. A hot meal was a luxury. Bed was a straw pallet up on deck. There was little protection from the weather. If your clothes were wet there was no way to

The leadsman

dry them, and you would have been plagued by lice and other vermin. There were no engines, no ship-to-shore telephones, no Coast Guard, no radar. There was only a compass, a quadrant, and the stars to steer by. And once you left the familiar coastline of your country, there were no landmarks. You heard tales of

You might never be heard from again.

sea monsters and sirens and mysterious storms. Some sailors never returned: Just a few years before Columbus's voyage, a group had sailed west from the Azores to find land and had never been heard from again.

Still, the sailing ships of 1492 were state-of-the-art craft for their time. Shipbuilders in Spain and Portugal had borrowed the best ideas from ships developed in various countries. The vessels had pumps and rudders, and each usually carried a small boat. They had maps and charts from previous voyages. And they could travel great distances. A Portuguese explorer by the name of Bartholomeu Dias had already sailed all the way down the coast of Africa and rounded the Cape of Good Hope. Explorers were eager to try new routes, and a certain number of adventurous sailors were willing to go with them. Everyone wanted the riches that were waiting over the horizon.

Columbus set sail the same day the last Jews left Spain.

This was the way things were when Christopher Columbus set out on his famous voyage. He outfitted three ships and hired two other captains and a crew of about ninety men.[26] There were cabin boys, or gromets, on all three ships. There were two of them on the *Santa María*, Columbus's flagship. (Both were named Pedro.) Because he was planning such a long voyage, Columbus had trouble getting sailors to sign on. He finally took on a few convicts, after promising them royal pardons when they returned. Martin Pinzón, the captain of the *Pinta*, promised *his* crew that they would find houses roofed with gold.

Columbus was probably one of the greatest navigators of his time. Still, when his ships first sailed out of sight of the Canary Islands, the men cried. After that Columbus kept a false set of charts to show the crew, so they wouldn't know how far they were going.[27] In spite of that, the men grew restless. He almost had a mutiny on his hands. They finally sighted the island of Guanahani on the morning of October 12. It was probably not a moment too soon.

Across the Ocean Sea

T here's a chain of islands off the coast of North America, south and east of Florida. Some of them, like the island of Cuba, are hundreds of miles long. Others, like Watling Island and Samana Cay, are no more than fly specks on the map.

One of those fly speck islands was called Guanahani by the people who lived there. In 1492, no one on the other side of the world knew it was there. But people had been living on that island chain since about 5000 B.C.E. They "owned" those green specks in the ocean, although they probably had no understanding of that idea.

In 1492 Guanahani was a place of flowering trees, sweet-smelling plants, and lush fruit. In the center of the island there was a lagoon of fresh water. Parrots filled the skies; the reefs

This European artist had never seen an iguana.

around the island were teeming with fish. On land there were iguanas, lizards, armadillos, and tropical birds. The people who lived on Guanahani were Lucayan/Taino people. They were tall. They had tanned skin and straight hair, which they wore short in a bang in front and long and knotted in the back. Their foreheads were broad and flat, possibly because of their custom of head-binding. They painted their bodies with black, red, and white dyes. They sometimes wore gold jewelry. Only the pregnant women wore clothing.

The Lucayan people of Guanahani built neat houses made of thatch and slept in woven nets of cotton suspended above the ground. They ate spicy dishes of fish and sweet potato. And they baked flat bread, which they made from manioc (cassava) root. The women were good farmers. But the lives of the Taino men were shaped by the sea. Their boats were works of art,

The Lucayans built large, handsome, wooden boats they called Kanawas.

large wooden canoes that could be paddled over the coral reefs at incredible speeds. Some of these *kanawas*, as they called them, could hold as many as fifty people. In them the Lucayans traveled from island to island to trade with other groups of Taino people on Cuba and on what we now call Haiti and the Dominican Republic.

The Lucayan and Taino groups shared a spoken language, *Arawakan*, and a culture. The custom of sleeping in a hammock comes directly from this group of people, whom Columbus described as "the gentlest people in the world."[28] Some of the words we use today also come from them: canoe, tobacco, hammock, iguana, hurricane, manatee, maize.

If you were a member of this culture in 1492, life was peaceful and leisurely. There was plenty of food to be had from the sea, and the warm weather and tropical rains were good for growing things. Girls and women wove baskets and textiles from fiber and cotton. Boys and men carved animal and flower figures on their ax handles. There was time for meetings and dances in the stone-fringed central plaza, which in Arawakan you would have called a *batey*. There was time to light the leaf of the aromatic tobacco plant and inhale the smoke and pass it around. And there were games played with balls. Both girls and boys played a form of soccer with a rubber ball.

There was a chief of your island village. He was carried around on a litter, sat on a special carved wooden seat, called a *duho*, and was entitled to have more than one wife. He took care of the everyday affairs of your village. But the more powerful matters were in the hands of the gods, like Baibrama, who represented good crops.

To keep yourself safe from harm, you and the other islanders might have worn a charm called a *zemi* around your neck. But, actually, there was very little to be afraid of. There were no dangerous animals on the islands and no people with guns. At the beginning of the year 1492, there were probably only two things to be afraid of on Guanahani and the neighboring islands. One was hurricanes. The other was the fierce Ciboney tribes that occasionally sent raiding parties from the interior of another island.

Then came October 11, 1492. You might have spent that day fishing from your canoe. Or perhaps you were busy weaving or carving a monkey on an ax handle. Or painting a piece of pottery. That evening you might have hunted crabs by the light of a torch. And then you would have curled up in your hammock and slept soundly, not knowing that the next day your life would be changed forever.

October 12, 1492: The strangers arrive.

Early on the morning of October 12, Christopher Columbus and his three ships sighted land. They anchored offshore of the island of Guanahani, which Columbus promptly named San Salvador. Some historians think this island was Watling Island, and some think it was Samana Cay. A party went ashore in small boats and exchanged gifts with the people they called "Indians." The Spaniards gave them colored beads and hawks' bells. The islanders gave the Spaniards gifts of gold; one of the chiefs later gave Columbus a mask with ears, tongue, and nose of gold. Columbus thought he had reached the Indies and that these people were natives of Cipangu (Japan).

There is no record of what the Lucayans thought.

What Happened after 1492 . . .

ABDALLAH, the defeated Moorish sultan, went into exile. A year later he was killed in Morocco fighting for the king of Fez. Within ten years, Ferdinand and Isabella had broken every promise they had made to the Arabs. About 300,000 Moors, including the *Moriscos*, who had converted to Christianity, were eventually forced to leave Spain.

The beautiful *ALHAMBRA* palace was partly dismantled, and a Catholic church was built over it. The Alhambra's priceless library of 80,000 Arab books was burned. But the door that Abdallah had ordered sealed remains that way to this day.

The teenage genius *MICHELANGELO* lived to become a famous artist in Italy. His work can still be seen today in famous buildings in Italy and in museums all over the world.

The *JEWS* had been excluded from all Europe by the end of the fifteenth century. They were forbidden to settle in any of the newly discovered lands. In spite of that, many Jews and *marranos* did go to the New World during the sixteenth century. Colonies of expelled Jews remained in Turkey, India, China, and the Middle East.

The *SPANISH INQUISITION* continued for 300 years, and the expulsion order against the Jews was not officially revoked by the Spanish government until December 16, 1968.

The globe that the mapmaker *MARTIN BEHAIM* made is still in existence. It stands in the National Museum in Nuremberg, Germany—the oldest globe on earth.

The *LUCAYANS* and other *TAINO* island people fell prey to disease and to Spanish exploitation. Thousands of them were shipped as slaves to Spain. Within twenty years they had been virtually wiped out.

On his first voyage, *CHRISTOPHER COLUMBUS* explored Cuba, Haiti, and several other Caribbean islands. He returned to Spain and was given a royal welcome by Isabella and

Ferdinand. He made three more voyages to the New World, visiting many of the islands of the West Indies and sailing down the coast of Central America as far as Panama. He died in 1506, still believing that the lands he had seen were a gateway to Asia.

QUEEN ISABELLA and *KING FERDINAND* lived long enough to see Spain become a major power in Europe and to claim territories in the New World. But Spain never fully recovered from the loss of her Jewish and Arab citizens, and her greedy exploitation of the New World finally caused her decline to a third-rate power.

Columbus showed off his Indian captives at court.

Notes

~~~~~~~~~~~

1. Fernand Braudel in his *Perspectives of History* gives the figure as near 300 million. The *Penguin Atlas of Modern History* says it was around 400 million. (In 1990 there were over 5 billion people in the world.)

In the fifteenth century, populations changed dramatically from one short period to another because of plagues. In 1492, for example, Europe was still recovering from a plague that had wiped out half its people.

2. Columbus wrote about his voyages. In one document he says he traveled to "an island larger than Thule." According to Robert Fuson (*The Log of Christopher Columbus*), Columbus made at least one voyage to England and perhaps one to Iceland.

3. King John is quoted as saying that he found Columbus to be "a big talker and boastful in setting forth his accomplishments." (See *The Discoverers*.)

4. The gentleman who compared Spanish inns to French pigpens is anonymous, but his remark is preserved. (See *The Spain of Ferdinand and Isabella*.)

5. Both potatoes and tomatoes were brought to Europe from the New World. Columbus saw sweet potatoes in the Caribbean in 1492. He also

brought back some maize on his first voyage. White potatoes first appeared in Spain about 1550 and were probably discovered in Peru. (See *Everyday Life in Renaissance Times*.)

6. Quoted in *The Golden Book of the Renaissance*.

7. There is evidence that Martin Pinzón, the captain of the *Pinta*, may have died of syphilis, which he'd contracted in the islands. (See *The Life and Times of Columbus*.)

8. In their struggle against Abdallah, the Spanish monarchs kidnapped the sultan's son. Later they tried to kidnap the son of their court physician and hold him as hostage. Ferdinand's own brother Charles, who was in line for the throne of Aragon, was stricken by a mysterious illness and died. Historians have speculated that he was poisoned. Isabella's brother Alfonso was found dead in his bed at the age of fourteen. (See *Ferdinand and Isabella*.) The history of these royal assassinations and kidnappings are preserved in such stories as "The Little Lame Prince."

9. Isabella imported teachers from Italy to tutor the court in poetry, philosophy, and other aspects of "the new learning" that was coming from Renaissance Italy. (See *The World Awakes*.)

10. It was customary for Isabella to travel to various parts of the country and to sit in the courts and listen to grievances. One source says she traveled throughout her kingdom for this purpose for the greater part of the year. Another source says she sat in on the courts "at least four times a year." It was obviously unusual for a monarch to be so directly in touch with her subjects. *Ferdinand and Isabella* offers the information that not only were each of her five children born in a different city; once her travels had exhausted her so thoroughly that she had a miscarriage.

11. According to his son Ferdinand, Columbus wrote a letter to Isabella and Ferdinand in 1501, in which he said, "Our Lord revealed to me that

it was feasible to sail from here to the Indies and placed in me a burning desire to carry out His plan." (See *The Life and Times of Christopher Columbus*.)

12. It was the model of Isabella that inspired Spanish women to "take an unusual share in the new studies. The queen's Latin teacher was a woman. Other women even lectured at the great Spanish universities." (See *The World Awakes*.)

13. Beating sense into a boy or girl was a recommended form of discipline all over Europe in 1492. An example is the father of the Paston family of England, who gave orders that his son Clement "be truly belashed" by his masters in London if he did not do well. (See *Private Life in the Fifteenth Century*.)

14. From *Timetables of History*, by Bernard Grun (New York: Touchstone, Simon & Schuster, 1979).

15. Isabella and Ferdinand had five children: four daughters and a son. All the children spoke Latin fluently and were educated to assume royal positions. Their daughter Catherine was the first wife of King Henry VIII of England.

16. Plantin's printing operation in Antwerp is well documented in several accounts of the period. By the beginning of the sixteenth century he had several hundred employees. This anecdote is from *Made in the Renaissance*.

17. Blindman's buff is a version of tag in which the person who is "it" is blindfolded. For more information on the games of children, see *Centuries of Childhood*.

18. The idea developed in what was then Germany that witchcraft was more natural to women than to men. As a result, while hundreds of men were killed in the witchcraft frenzy, *thousands* of women were killed. This notion persisted for hundreds of years, even in the New World. Spain,

however, was not particularly infected by it. (See *Everyday Life in Renaissance Times*.)

19. Some pictures of these accusations have been preserved; see *The Spain of Ferdinand and Isabella*.

20. Several historians have questioned the way Columbus presented himself. The strongest argument for his vagueness about his background seems to be that he was trying to hide something. Either he had Jewish ancestry (a liability in Spain), or his family had been involved politically in some issue that was best covered up. (See *The Log of Christopher Columbus*; also *Spain in America*.)

21. The account of this meeting between Abravanel (also called Abarbanel) and Torquemada appears in several sources, among them *Abarbanel and the Expulsion of the Jews from Spain*, by Jacob S. Minkin (New York: Behrman's Jewish Book House, 1938).

22. The numbers of displaced Jews vary from one historical account to another. Simon Wiesenthal (*Sails of Hope*) estimates it at about 200,000. Historians are pretty much agreed that the number was well over 100,000.

23. Abraham Zacuto was one of the most respected cartographers of his time and the author of a book on navigation, which Columbus appears to have owned and studied. Zacuto was forced to leave Spain in 1492 under the expulsion order.

24. See *National Geographic*, November 1986.

25. The ship's speed for a short distance was plotted by dropping a chip of wood overboard and timing it with a chant. But navigating by dead reckoning required an instrument that could measure the passage of longer intervals of time. The sandglass was well suited for this purpose. The course was plotted on a board every half hour and compass bearings were entered. Totals were entered at the end of each four-hour watch and then added up

at the end of twelve hours. From these figures a good sailor could calculate distance made good. If the sandglass was not turned on time, the error would accumulate. (See *The Log of Christopher Columbus*.)

26. There is general agreement that Columbus's three ships carried between 87 and 90 men. The *Santa Maria* probably had 40, the *Pinta* 26, the *Niña* 24. (See *The Log of Christopher Columbus*.)

27. In his log, Columbus mentions several times minimizing the distance he had traveled. In his entry of September 10, 1492, he says, "Today I made 180 miles at a speed of 7½ knots. I recorded only 144 miles in order not to alarm the sailors if the voyage is lengthy." (See *The Log of Christopher Columbus*.)

28. Of the people of the islands, Columbus said, "The entire country is inhabited by very good and gentle people." And in another place, he says, "Your Highness may believe that in all the world there cannot be better or more gentle people." In spite of his warm feelings for the Lucayan Arawaks, Columbus did take seven prisoners to bring back to Spain. One of them jumped overboard from the *Santa Maria* and escaped. (See *The Log of Christopher Columbus*.)

Bibliography

Ariès, Philippe. *Centuries of Childhood: A Social History of Family Life*. Translated by Robert Baldick. New York: Knopf, 1962.

Boorstin, Daniel J. *The Discoverers*. New York: Random House, 1983.

Bourne, Edward Gaylord. *Spain in America, 1450–1580*. Vol. 3 of *The American Nation: A History*. New York: Harper & Brothers, 1904.

Bradford, Ernle. *Christopher Columbus*. New York: Viking Press, 1973.

Braudel, Fernand. *The Perspective of the World*. Vol. 3 of *Civilization and Capitalism: 15th–18th Century*. Translated by Siân Reynolds. New York: Harper & Row, 1982.

———. *The Structures of Everyday Life: The Limits of the Possible*. Vol. 1 of *Civilization and Capitalism: 15th–18th Century*. Translated by Siân Reynolds. New York: Harper & Row, 1981.

Brooks, Polly Schoyer, and Nancy Zinsser Walworth. *The World Awakes: The Renaissance in Western Europe*. Philadelphia: J. B. Lippincott, 1962.

Cardini, Franco. *Europe 1492: Portrait of a Continent Five Hundred Years Ago*. New York: Facts on File, 1989.

Chamberlin, Eric Russell. *Everyday Life in Renaissance Times*. New York: Putnam, 1966.

Crow, John A. *Spain, the Root and the Flower: A History of the Civilization of Spain and of the Spanish People*. New York: Harper & Row, 1963.

Fuson, Robert H. *The Log of Christopher Columbus*. Camden, Maine: International Marine, 1987.

Giardini, Cesare. *The Life and Times of Columbus*. Translated by Arnaldo Mondadori. Curtis Internationale, 1967.

Grant, Neil. *The Renaissance*. New York: Franklin Watts, 1971.

Grun, Bernard. *The Timetables of History: A Horizontal Linkage of People and Events*. New York: Simon & Schuster, 1979.

Harrison, Molly. *Children in History*. Book I, *The Middle Ages*. London: Hulton Educational Pub., 1959.

Editors of *Horizon Magazine* and Melveena McKendrick. *Ferdinand and Isabella*. New York: American Heritage, 1968.

Jewish Life and Literature: A Collection of Pamphlets. New York: New York Public Library, 1979. Microfiche.

Judge, Joseph, Luis Marden, and Eugene Lyon. "Columbus and the New World." *National Geographic*, November 1986, 562–605.

Mariéjol, Jean Hippolyte. *The Spain of Ferdinand and Isabella*. Translated and edited by Benjamin Keen. New Brunswick, N.J.: Rutgers University Press, 1961.

Milanich, Jerald T., and Susan Milbrath, eds. *First Encounters: Spanish Explorations in the Caribbean and the United States, 1492–1570*. Gainesville, Fla.: University Presses of Florida, 1989.

Minkin, Jacob S. *Abarbanel and the Expulsion of the Jews from Spain*. New York: Behrman's Jewish Book House, 1938.

Morison, Samuel Eliot. *Admiral of the Ocean Sea: A Life of Christopher Columbus*. Boston: Northeastern University Press, 1983.

Price, Christine. *Made in the Renaissance: Arts and Crafts of the Age of Exploration*. New York: Dutton, 1963.

Shapiro, Irwin. *The Golden Book of the Renaissance*. Adapted from *The Horizon Book of the Renaissance* by the editors of *Horizon Magazine* and J. H. Plumb. New York: Golden Press, 1962.

Virgoe, Roger, ed. *Private Life in the Fifteenth Century*. London: Weidenfeld and Nicolson UK, 1989.

Wallace, Robert, and the editors of Time-Life Books. *The World of Leonardo: 1452–1519*. New York: Time Inc., 1966.

Weber, Eugen. *A Modern History of Europe: Men, Cultures, and Societies from the Renaissance to the Present*. New York: Norton, 1971.

Wiesenthal, Simon. *Sails of Hope: The Secret Mission of Christopher Columbus*. New York: Macmillan, 1973.

Wilford, John Noble. *The Mapmakers*. New York: Knopf, 1981.

Picture Credits

Half-title and pages 12, 28, 55, 57, 66, 79, 84, and 95: The Bettmann Archive

Page vi: From *Canzone per Andare in Machera per Carneschiale,* by Lorenzo de Medici (ca. 1497)

Page 2: Etching of Genoa from 1486

Page 4: Mercator projection of Martin Behaim's map (Fiske, 1902)

Pages 6–7: Detail from Bernhard Breitenbach's *Journey to the Holy Land*, Mainz 1486

Page 8: Map by Cathy Bobak

Page 11 and throughout: 1575 engraving by Tobias Stimmer from an original (ca. 1550)

Pages 15, 21, and 68: Courtesy Spanish Tourist Bureau

Page 19: New York Public Library Picture Collection. After original by B. Mercadé in Gerona Provincial Archaeological Museum

Pages 24–25: New York Public Library Picture Collection

Page 31: From *De Gli Habiti Antichi,* by Vecellio, 1590

Pages 34 and 39: Old engravings. Originals in British Museum, London

Page 35: From a medical textbook of 1493

Page 45: From a Florentine spelling primer (ca. 1500)

Page 47: Original in Colegiata: Toro

Page 50: From a Florentine book on chess written 1493 by Jacopo Cessolis

Pages 52 and 53: DaVinci Parachute, Coc. Atl. folio 381 V-A Fuselage of Flying Machine-MS. B, folio 74 V

Page 56: From the edition of Marco Polo's travels owned by Columbus. Original in Columbian Library, Seville

Page 59: From 16th-century German engraving of an auto da fé. Original in Bibliotheque National, Paris

Page 73: Ptolemaic map of 1493

Page 74: Courtesy German National Museum, Nuremberg

Pages 77 and 82: From Olaus Magnus, *Historia de Gentibus Septentrionalibus,* 1555

Page 81: Title page of an English book about mariners (ca. 1550)

Page 87: From Oviedo's *Historia,* 1547

Page 88: From *Historia del Muondo Nuovo,* by Gerolamo Benzoni, 1542

Page 91: Original in Ducal Palace, Genoa

Index

Page numbers in italics indicate illustrations.

de Nebrija, Antonio (writer), 54
de Torquemada, Tomás (Isabella's religious adviser)
  and the expulsion of the Jews, *66*
  and the Spanish Inquisition, 60–61, 64
Dias, Bartholomeu (explorer), 83
diseases, 33–36, 96
doctors, of medicine, *34,* 34–36, *35*

education. *See also* books
  of boys, 39–40, 44, 46
  of girls, 40, 46–48
  levels of, 43–44
  in royal court, 40, 97
  for war, 39, 46
  of women, 43, *47,* 98
entertainment, 49–50, *50*
  of Lucayans, 89
Europe, 4–7. *See also* names of countries; specific topics
explorers, 5, 10–11, 83. *See also* diseases spread by, 36
  and maps, 71–72, 75
farms and farming. *See* agriculture
Ferdinand, King. *See* Isabella, Queen, and King Ferdinand
food
  aboard ships, 32, 81
  of Lucayans, 88–89
  of Spain, 26–27
  table manners, *28, 29*

games. *See* entertainment
Genoa, Italy, *2,* 11
Germany, 60, 72, 94, 99
globes. *See* maps and globes
Glockenthon (artist), 72–73
government
  by kings, queens, and nobles, 37–41
  of Lucayans, 90
Grenada. *See* Alhambra
Guanahani, island of
  arrival of Columbus on, 85, 92
  people of, 86–92

health. *See* diseases
Henry the Navigator (ruler of Portugal), 37
houses. *See* architecture

Indians. *See* Lucayans
Indies, the, 7, 12, 42, 70, 94–95
inns, of Spain, 15–16
Inquisition, Spanish, 60–64
  end of, 94
  victims of, *59, 62*
Isabella, Queen, and King Ferdinand, 9–10, 37–42, *39*
  after 1492, 95
  children of, 98–99
  and Columbus, 23, 42, 94–95
  and the Jews, 66–67
  and the Moors, 22–23, *24–25,* 93
  rule of, 14–15, 37–42, 97, 98

Italy, *vi,* 51, 97. *See also* Genoa; Medici family; Michelangelo; Venice

Japan (Cipangu), 5, 75, 92
Jews, 18
  expulsion of, 64–70, *69,* 94
  and Isabella, 42
  and the Moors, 20
  roles and influence of, 36, 71, 95
  and the Spanish Inquisition, 61–64, 65
John, King of Portugal, and Columbus, 12

kings, 12, 37–41. *See also* Isabella, Queen, and King Ferdinand

language(s)
  Arawakan, 89
  of Columbus, 48
  in Spain, 40, 46, 54
Lucayans
  after arrival of Columbus, *91,* 92, 94, *95,* 101
  life of, 86–90
maps and globes, *73*
  making of, 71, 72–75
  Martin Behaim's, *74,* 94
  mistakes on, 3–4, *4,* 71, 75
marriage, 47, 68, 90
medical care, *34,* 34–36, *35*
Medici family (rulers of Florence, Italy), 37, 51
Michelangelo, Buonarroti (artist), 51, 93